Introduction

A popular song of some years ago had the lyrics, "those hazy, lazy, crazy days of summer." Every school-age child identified with those lyrics and every adult, upon hearing the song, remembered those carefree days. Memorial Day weekend until Labor Day was a time of freedom, of sheer joy for being out of school. The worst thing that could happen to a youngster was to have to attend summer school with its remedial and make-up courses, with classes hurriedly planned, with little thought being given to teacher selection or curriculum.

All this is changing; summer school is coming of age. In this fastback the reader will learn about what summer school has been and what it can be, about how it can offer something not only for the student with learning problems but also for the ambitious student and for the gifted and talented student.

Summer school has not received its rightful place in the educational world. It is now about to become an integral part of the total school system.

Historical Beginnings

The school year in American schools has historically followed a rigid schedule set by professional and community expectations. Parents expect their students to be home and free from school during the summer months. Teachers expect to be free during the summer to pursue further education, to travel, or simply to rest.

Conventional thinking of what a typical school year should be has tended to center around our heritage as an agrarian society. Children provided economical labor for the family farm or business. Even though some importance was attached to education, it was not permitted to interfere with the agricultural pursuits or business interests of the family. Thus, the school year lasted from the time the crops were harvested until it was time to plant again. This was usually late in the fall until early springtime.

As young people left the farms for the cities and as immigrants flocked to the U.S., the number of youths roaming the streets caused some alarm among the city fathers. With the passage of the first child labor law in 1916, school-age students had little, if anything, to do during the summer. Community leaders demanded that something be done to make better use of students' time during the summer. School officials responded first by developing recreational programs. Even today, advocates of the extended school year support recreational programs as a worthwhile objective for summer school.[1]

In addition to keeping the students off the streets, summer school was seen by educators as an opportunity to provide remediation to slower students. The wealthy were able to hire tutors if their children failed to achieve. The first summer programs were primarily for the

STBACK

8

Summer School: A New Look

John W. Dougherty

PHI DELTA KAPPA
EDUCATIONAL FOUNDATION

JOHN W. DOUGHERTY

John W. Dougherty is principal of Hazelwood Junior High School in Florissant, Missouri, where he also serves as the director of the gifted program for the junior high schools in the Hazelwood School District. Dougherty received his B.S. at Southwest Missouri State University, his M.S.T. at University of Missouri and his Ph.D. at St. Louis University. He has been visiting professor and extension instructor for Southeast Missouri State University for the last five years. He is presently serving as an evening mathematics instructor for the St. Louis Community College District.

Dr. Dougherty's articles on education have appeared in *NASSP Bulletin, Clearinghouse, School and Community, Phi Delta Kappan,* and other journals.

Series Editor, Derek L. Burleson

Summer School: A New Look

By John W. Dougherty

Library of Congress Catalog Card Number: 81-80016
ISBN 0-87367-158-9

Bloomington, Indiana

This fastback is sponsored by the Long Island New York Chapter of Phi Delta Kappa, which made a generous contribution toward publication costs. The chapter sponsors the fastback to honor Miss Bessie Gabbard, a member of the Board of Governors of the Phi Delta Kappa Educational Foundation.

TABLE OF CONTENTS

Introduction 7

Historical Beginnings 8

Summer School for the Failing Student
and Special Student 11

Summer School for the Ambitious Student 17

Summer School for the Gifted Student 19

The Year-Round School—A Summer Option 22

Administering the Summer School 25

References 29

poor. Some of the stigma still attached to summer schools is a result of that caste system. These early attempts at summer school programs were in the eastern part of the country.

A U.S. government study reported in 1841 that 11-month school calendars were being used in Baltimore, Buffalo, Cincinnati, Detroit, New York, Philadelphia, and Washington. Bluffton, Indiana, in 1904, became the first district to adopt the 12-month quarter plan.[2] So the idea of some form of school during the summer months is not new. The idea has persisted in a variety of forms since the turn of the century. Nevertheless, the nine-month school year is still the predominant pattern in the public schools.

Teachers and their professional organizations argue that teaching is an emotional strain and that some time is needed in the summer to recoup for the next school year. Administrators firmly state that it takes three months for them to refurbish the schools and prepare for the next group of students. Parents wish to have their children free to take on vacations, perform needed tasks around the house, work in the family business, etc. Most students agree with the teachers that they also need a three-month rest!

Attendance in summer school has usually been voluntary. If students did not wish to go to summer school, it was not demanded that they do so. They were either given a social promotion or retained in the present grade. With the advent of social promotions there was little need for a youngster to attend summer school. Those that attended did so because their parents were wise enough to realize that if their child was having difficulty in some subjects, summer school could help.

In 1959 James B. Conant published his influential *The American High School*. One of his recommendations was that boards of education provide a summer school not only for those who needed to repeat a subject but also for the bright and ambitious students who might wish to broaden the scope of their elective programs. Conant was concerned that academically talented students be given the opportunity to take such practical courses as typing and additional academic subjects if they so desired. His influence upon educators resulted in looking anew at a summer school that would include types of courses other than those needed for failing students.

With the increased enrollments during the 1950s and 1960s, some school administrators envisioned summer school as a means of accelerating students so that they could graduate early, thus making more room in the schools for additional youngsters. This idea never achieved wide acceptance, and few students ever took advantage of it, but it does have merit.

The massive amount of federal funding that came with passage of the Elementary and Secondary School Act in 1965 encouraged the schools to broaden their summer school programs. Accelerated math and science programs, foreign language programs, and remedial reading programs at the elementary level were all products of the federal dollar, and many of these programs were implemented through summer school offerings.

Educators, concerned about the wise use of leisure time, saw summer school as an opportunity to increase the students' interest in lifelong activities. Summer sports camps sponsored by school districts, often in conjunction with municipal recreational departments, were able to make use of the physical education facilities for a longer period of time. Music camps, summer drama presentations, and other educational leisure time pursuits also have come to be popular summer school activities.

This brief history highlights some of the influences that have changed the role of summer school in U.S. education. In the chapters that follow, we shall see in greater detail how the summer school can take on an expanded role and become an integral part of our school system.

Summer School for the Failing Student and Special Student

The conventional image of summer schools persists as a program for pupils who need to make up one or more failed courses or for those needing remedial work to keep pace with their classmates. It is still a legitimate function of summer school to assist youngsters who have difficulty during the school year. There are three groups of students in this category that the summer school can serve: 1) the student lacking minimal basic skills, 2) the student who needs summer school to fulfill the objectives written into an individualized education program (IEP), now required under the Education for All Handicapped Children Act (PL.94-142), and 3) the student who needs more time to achieve success.

Minimum Basic Skills Student

By 1978, 33 states had mandated, in some form or other, minimum educational standards as a requirement for graduation or promotion.[3] The remaining states had studies underway or pending legislation. Minimum competency tests are generally administered in the last months of the school year on the assumption that a student will be more proficient at that time in those areas in which a competency level is required. Regardless of the level of minimal competency, there will be some youngsters who will not be able to pass the test the first time it is given. This will create immense pressure for expensive remedial work. The summer school provides opportunity for the schools to meet the challenge.

Those students who fail the minimum competency test could be offered the opportunity in summer school to achieve the skills they need. Obviously, if the student has not mastered the skills needed during the regular school year using conventional teaching techniques, it would be foolish to use those same procedures during the summer. Summer school provides a rich opportunity to try out new curriculum as well as new teaching methods. For example, a youngster lacking basic computational skills could be taught to compensate for this deficiency by using a calculator. Here is an opportunity to pilot a curriculum innovation and at the same time help the student.

Students who are weak in writing need plenty of time to write, think about what they have written, and write again. During the regular school day there is often not the time to do the writing and rewriting necessary to achieve proficiency. In summer school enough time could be devoted to writing to help students achieve an acceptable level of competency.

Some minimum competency tests require a student to show proficiency in certain life skills—filling out a job application or income tax form, understanding a credit agreement, etc. It is possible that a student could not demonstrate competency in these skills by means of a written test. Under such circumstances, it seems reasonable to offer some plan whereby the student could demonstrate on-the-job competency during the summer months. A teacher would then have time to observe his or her performance. This is presently done in some high school cooperative education programs.

Summer school offers the chance to provide a one-to-few or a one-to-one pupil/teacher ratio for students needing help on minimal basic requirements. Although most districts cannot afford such a pupil/teacher ratio during the regular school year, summer school classes are usually smaller so more individualization is possible.

Individualized Education Program Student

Under Public Law 94-142 every handicapped student is guaranteed the right to an appropriate free public education. To insure that the education is appropriate, an individualized education program (IEP) must be written and periodically updated. The important points of an IEP are the setting of long-term goals and short-term objectives, and they are to be carried out in the least restrictive environment. Most IEPs are written in the fall of the year by teachers in consultation with the parents and, in some cases, with the students themselves. The short-term objectives are those that can be met within several months or a semester. The long-term goals are those that can be met by the end of a school year.

In June 1979 U.S. District Judge Clarence Newcomer ruled that the Pennsylvania Department of Education must provide a program beyond the normal 180-day school year for any handicapped youngster who needs it. The ruling was based on the premise that handicapped youngsters may regress if their educational progress is interrupted during the summer months. This ruling has been upheld by the Third U.S. Circuit Court of Appeals in an August 1980 decision.

The implications of this court ruling are relevant to every school district. If there are handicapped students needing to attend summer school to attain their long-range goals, then the districts are going to have to provide the appropriate summer school experiences. There are few school districts that currently offer summer school programs for the handicapped. If schools are to respond to this court ruling, then they will need to employ special education teachers in all areas over the summer. Also counselors will need to be included on the summer staff to work with handicapped youngsters who have emotional and socialization problems. Equipment, supplies, and apparatus normally stored over the summer will need to be kept in continuous use. Bus drivers will need to be kept on to provide transportation for the handicapped to and from school as well as for field trips.

In the *Journal of Learning Disabilities* (March 1979), Saroj Sutaria cites the following rationale for the learning disabled student in a summer school program.

1. To provide a continuum of services to learning disabled children.

2. To provide a head start for some children.

3. To reinforce prior learning that otherwise would be forgotten.

4. To provide parents the opportunity to observe children gaining in self-confidence, which improves self-concept.

5. Small class size and relaxed atmosphere with patient and under-

standing teachers contribute to children having better self-control, greater willingness to share and be cooperative, and greater tolerance of others' difficulties.

6. Field trips and Special Olympics participation provide needed motivation and diversion from the academic program.[4]

Since P.L. 94-142 requires handicapped students to have equal educational opportunities, then the privilege of attending summer school is also theirs. Clearly, summer schools will present many new challenges to their administrators.

Failing Student

Youngsters fail during the school year for many reasons: absenteeism due to illness, laziness, poor study habits, disruptive home life, emotional traumas, and in some cases, a combination of these.

Chris, a very intelligent eighth-grade student, missed nearly half of the school year. Consequently, she failed and was required to attend summer school to make up the required courses. This she readily did without missing a single day. Her explanation was simple. She was absent approximately 80 days during the school year but was able to make them up by attending 30 days of summer school, thus gaining a net of 50 days. She made the system work for her very effectively.

However, most students who fail are not like Chris. They fail because they are unable to study effectively or to structure their time in order to get the work turned in on schedule. They are the ones who forget to study for a test, lose their assignments, cannot find the text book, etc. Consequently, they receive a failing grade. Their failure is due to poor organization, not necessarily a lack of academic ability.

Jack failed literature and poetry. He felt that these were subjects beneath his masculine dignity. He had to make up the class during summer school. The summer school teacher, not knowing Jack, assumed that students who have failed English needed the basics, so she concentrated on grammar, spelling, and writing. Jack passed his English course in summer school easily because he had a good foundation in the basics, but nothing was done in summer school to correct his deficiency in literature and poetry. Kevin failed percents and decimals but passed in summer school because it covered the fundamental operations of addition, subtraction, multiplication, and division. Many school districts are beginning to look at this problem of addressing the real deficiencies of failing students in order to make summer school a more educationally sound experience.

To repeat what has been attempted in the normal school year, within a shorter time span, using the same curriculum, the same teaching techniques, and the same teacher/pupil ratio—all under the guise of remediation—doesn't make sense. Summer school should not be a carbon copy of the regular school year. When a student fails, diagnostic steps should be taken to ascertain the reasons why. Diagnostic data might include the teacher's evaluation, standardized test scores (if available), and other testing information. This information should be compiled and given to the summer school teacher. The students would be taught those things in which they are deficient and not retaught that which they already know.

There is mounting criticism of the long established policy in many school districts of social promotions, which is likely to have an impact on summer schools. Teachers are no longer under pressure to socially promote a student. Since teachers are held accountable for students' progress, they establish their standards; and any student unable to meet these is subject to failure. The student is told either to repeat the grade or course or to attend summer school. Most parents will prefer that their child enroll in summer school rather than face the stigma of being a grade behind, even though this stigma is slowly disappearing as the number of students being retained increases.

Can summer school be a viable alternative to retention? Research on retention would indicate that it is worth a try. Clair Koons states, "There is considerable research indicating . . . that nonpromoted children do not progress as far as do their regularly promoted counterparts." She also cites research that questions the assumption that a skill not learned the first time will be learned the next time the performance is repeated.[5] Also, as long ago as 1911, Charles Henry Keyes reported that of a large number of retained students in one school district, 20% did better, 39% showed no change, and 40% actually did worse.[6] Based on these studies and others, it would appear that retaining students does not necessarily improve their chances for success. If summer school is an alternative, it must be a different type of program from that which failing students have had during the regular school year.

Clearly, parental pressure in the last decade has shifted from one of "promote my child" to one of "make him learn." Lawsuits challenging school districts for promoting and graduating students who are functionally illiterate have received widespread media coverage in the past few years. While to date parents have not won these cases, they do indicate that parents and the public hold the schools accountable for turning out high school graduates with at least minimum skills. Summer school offers a second chance for the student who has not been able to succeed in the normal school program.

Summer School for the Ambitious Student

There are many students who cannot partake of all the offerings in a large comprehensive high school because there is not enough time in their schedules. Many students in college preparatory programs would like to pursue their interests in industrial arts, cooking, sewing, or other avocational or vocational areas; but the academic load is too demanding to permit them to participate in these non-academic areas. Summer school provides an opportunity for these students to pursue these interests.

It is true, these special interest courses normally have not been offered in summer school. They are expensive; there are usually not enough students to justify them; and staffing is difficult because teachers in these areas can get better paying summer jobs due to their technical skills. However, some schools have solved this problem by using a "back-door" method. They offer the required academic courses for these students during the summer. Students then have time during the regular school year for those avocational courses that have high interest for them.

Summer school can also serve the student who is heavily involved in extracurricular programs during the school year. Students who serve in student government, drama productions, interscholastic sports, and community service projects have such busy schedules that their time for studying is limited. By carrying a smaller class load during the regular year they can fully participate in extracurricular activities and pick up required courses during the summer.

There are some students who wish to complete high school early in order to pursue other interests. A common attitude among high school seniors is that the last year is a waste of time, except for having a good time. Many high schools now allow students to graduate early if they have the necessary credits and if they have definite plans for college or other post high school plans. For example, students may wish to start college following their junior year or first semester of their senior year. By accumulating the required Carnegie units in summer school, a student may skip the senior year and still graduate. Skipping the senior year also permits early entrance into military service, trade schools, apprenticeships, etc.

Many students in work-study programs such as cooperative office education, distributive education, health occupations, etc., use summer school to accumulate academic credits so they can concentrate on their work-study job during the regular school year. In many cases they are able to start work during the summer school term and retain the job as a work-study assignment when school begins in the fall.

Ideally, summer school should make available all the normal curricular offerings. Practically, this is not possible. However, if there are enough required academic subjects available, a student may take these, thus freeing up time during the regular school year for extracurricular activities, work-study, and special interest courses.

Summer School for the Gifted Student

Frequently programs for the gifted and talented are scheduled outside the regular school day. Because of the pressures of time, many gifted students do not participate in the very programs designed for them. A case in point is a fifth-grade girl who pleaded with her parents and teacher not to put her in the gifted program, even though she was well-qualified. The extra work coupled with piano lessons and practice, Girl Scouts, church youth group, etc., did not leave her any time to be just a fifth-grade girl. Fortunately, her parents were wise enough to recognize the time pressures on their child and acceded to her wishes. For students like this gifted fifth grader, summer school can provide the time for a variety of enrichment activities that will challenge her talents.

There is now considerable support from both state and federal sources for school systems to develop programs for the gifted (see fastback #119 *Teaching the Gifted and Talented*). Many schools have responded by accelerating bright students, by offering advanced-placement courses, or by developing a variety of after-school or weekend programs. While all these efforts have merit, they tend to isolate the gifted and remove them from normal socialization experiences with their peers, which all children need. Summer school can offer some exciting options for gifted and talented students without the unreasonable time pressures they face during the regular school year.

Three approaches have been used in summer programs for the gifted: 1) advanced courses, 2) utilizing community resources, and 3) special programs for the gifted. These approaches are not always conducted under the administration of the regular summer school, but the school district has a role in coordinating and publicizing these opportunities for the gifted.

Advanced courses. As an alternative to acceleration, which separates gifted students from their age group, academically talented students can be encouraged to take advanced courses offered in summer school. Math and science courses, in particular, have strong appeal for these students. For the artistically talented student, the summer school can offer them opportunities to work in a variety of media and with specialist teachers or craft persons not generally available in the regular art curriculum. Other special interest summer courses such as creative writing, humanities, communications, and photography are popular with the gifted and can challenge their talents.

Because summer school attracts a wide age range of students from many sections of the community, gifted students have an opportunity to interact with those both older and younger than themselves and those from a variety of backgrounds. Associating with other gifted students helps talented youngsters to assess their capabilities more realistically.

Utilizing community resources. Whether conducted by the school district or by other agencies in the community, summer programs that utilize the resources of the community have much to offer the gifted and talented. Museums, zoos, nature preserves, and planetariums offer their own programs that appeal to the interests of many gifted students. These institutions might also work cooperatively with the local schools in tailoring a special summer program for the gifted.

For those gifted in the performing arts, many communities offer summer orchestras and bands, drama and musical comedy productions, and dance groups. A variety of apprenticeships might be arranged for students interested in law, journalism, or computer science, to name a few. Whether or not students receive pay and/or academic credit for their work, these kinds of experiences expose gifted students to future career options and give them a taste of what the working world is really like.

Special programs for the gifted. Many schools and colleges now sponsor special summer programs for gifted and talented students. In addition to offering worthwhile programs, colleges see these summer events as a way to utilize their facilities and to recruit future students. Some of the more popular college workshops are in the areas of sports, leadership, science, math, and journalism.

Public schools offer a variety of special summer programs for the gifted. In a directory published by Mars Hill College[7] over 25 summer programs are listed for the gifted. Some examples are:

Your Wonderful Imagination. Charlotte-Mecklenburg School District in Charlotte, N.C., has a program designed for grades 4, 5, & 6 where the students use their imagination to investigate life from cavemen to space travel.

Enhancement '79. Houston Schools in Warner Robins, Ga., offer a total of 28 courses in the fine arts, academics, and psychology for ages 10 to 12.

Summer Program of Special Interest and Fine Arts. Winston-Salem/Forsythe Schools in Winston Salem, N.C., offer a program of enrichment and stimulation over 14 areas, including a camping trip, for ages 7 to 15.

As school systems continue to develop programs for the gifted, they should include summer school in their plans. Schools need not duplicate the many excellent programs already available in the community. Rather, they should counsel gifted students to take advantage of these opportunities.

The Year-Round School—A Summer Option

Many who see school buildings empty for 25% of the year have questioned the traditional nine-month school year of 180 days divided into two semesters. While many communities use school facilities for summer recreational programs and other activities, the fact remains that most school buildings are under-utilized during the summer months. A variety of schemes have been proposed for a year-round school or an extended school year that make use of school buildings during the summer. Among the various plans are:

Extended Summer School. This plan is a make-up school whereby students may retake those courses they have failed during the regular school year, or it provides an opportunity for students to take courses and graduate from high school early. The Syosset Plan is an example of an extended summer school where a student may graduate a year early.[8]

Trimester Plan. This plan is similar to the extended summer school except that the school year is divided into three sessions of equal time, including the summer session. A student may elect to attend any two of the three semesters or all three.[9]

Multiple Session Plan. Under this plan the entire year is divided into a number of equal sessions. A student must attend the required number of sessions or may elect to attend all of them. This plan provides opportunities to retake failed courses, to take courses for additional graduation credits, or to extend the normal course load over a longer period of time. The latter feature is very beneficial to a slow learner who may need additional time. The John Dewey High School in New York City has used this plan with a schedule of five seven-week cycles with an optional sixth summer cycle.[10]

Quarter Plan. This plan divides the year into four quarters. The students attend three out of four quarters, so they still have a three-month vacation; but the school district is able to accommodate 25% more students. This plan is more commonly used at the college level with Dartmouth College being perhaps the best known. Originally this plan was devised to ease overcrowded schools, but it has educational benefits as well.

Advocates of year-round schools or the extended school year give the following reasons for the plan:

1. To make better use of costly plant facilities that are unused for 25% of the year;
2. To improve the curriculum by pilot testing innovative programs;
3. To prevent loss of basic skills due to three-month vacation gap;
4. To reduce the number of buildings necessary to house the entire student body;
5. To reduce juvenile delinquency by having students in school during the summer;
6. To provide curriculum enrichment programs;
7. To provide teacher employment during the summer months;
8. To provide additional assistance for disadvantaged students, handicapped students, or slow learners;
9. To permit acceleration of the gifted/talented student;
10. To improve educational achievement.

To be honest, the educational justifications of year-round schools have often been secondary to the economics of housing more students in existing structures. With a year-round school calendar the number of students that can be housed is increased 25% over the number housed in a nine-month school year. Thus, on a per-pupil expenditure the cost of the building is reduced by one-fourth.

With declining enrollments, most school districts no longer face a shortage of buildings. They now must deal with the problem of what to do with empty buildings. In a relatively short period, the principal motivation for the year-round school—housing more students in existing facilities—has disappeared.

Once again, a new motivation unrelated to the education program is causing school administrations to take another look at the year-round school—the conservation of energy. Some school districts have examined the possibility of scheduling the traditional three-month summer vacation during December, January, and February. This would substantially reduce heating bills, but in warmer climates air conditioning would be required during the hot summer months. Air conditioning costs equal, if not exceed, fuel costs; so the energy saving would not be that substantial, at least not in the southern half of the country.

J. Jackson Barnette has proposed a new national calendar for education.[11] The plan includes about 34 weeks for traditional programming and about 18 weeks for vacation and nontraditional programming. The vacation and nontraditional programming would occur during mid-winter and mid-summer months. The 34 weeks would provide for 170 days, some of which would be taken by traditional holidays. To compensate for the fact that this calendar does not meet the 180-day legal requirement of most states, the school day could be lengthened by 10% or about 30 minutes. This new calendar might save as much as 15% to 20% in heating costs in the colder states. The decrease in number of school days would also permit a saving in transportation cost.

Enthusiasm for the year-round school or extended school year has definitely waned in the past few years. In the early Seventies Harold G. Shane and Owen N. Nelson conducted a poll of administrators and teachers which showed that 84% believed that by the mid-Eighties schools would be open 12 months and students' programs would be so individualized that they could leave school for three months each year, choosing both the time and length of vacation.[12] This has not occurred and there seems to be little likelihood that it will.

For the near future, the mainstay of the summer educational program is likely to be the traditional summer school. The present challenge is to make the summer school an integral part of the school's administrative structure. The next section will deal with administering the summer school.

Administering the Summer School

The summer school should receive the same administrative care and planning as the regular school year receives. Summer school can and must be more than babysitting a group of potential dropouts and the handing out of busy work. Summer school should not be an instant replay of the regular school year, especially if it is primarily for failing students.

Staffing

The key staff person for a summer school is the administrator. Too often the summer school principal is a rookie, who is given the assignment to gain experience for a future administrative post in the system. Beginning administrators have enough problems in running a building with an established staff. Since the summer school staff have little time for planning and are together for only six to eight weeks, the summer is not the time to train a beginning administrator.

The ideal person to administer the summer school is a district level administrator, who might also be responsible for adult education and community workshops. This individual is usually an experienced administrator who knows the system and has experience running programs other than the regular school program.

The summer teaching staff must be chosen with great care. If students have failed a course, repeating the same assignments from the previous year over a shorter time period is not going to be successful. Thus, teachers must be selected who will use new approaches for this type of summer school student.

With declining enrollments that result in reduction in force (RIF) actions, administrators should consider summer school as an opportunity to utilize good staff members who may have to be terminated otherwise.

Teachers should be given plenty of lead time to apply for summer school positions. When programming for summer school is made too late, good teachers may not be available because they have made other plans. Once the applications are received, the principal with whom the teacher works should be contacted for recommendations and other pertinent information. Teacher subject preference, certification standards, and district seniority are also factors that must be considered in selecting staff.

Ideally, teachers should be assigned to their own buildings. Practically, this is not usually possible since student enrollment does not justify the operation of more than one building at each level. The administrator should conduct an orientation for the summer school faculty to acquaint them with the building in which they will be working. This orientation will alleviate the concern of building principals about vandalism in their building by students who may not feel that they "belong" there.

Financing

Most summer schools are self-supporting. That is, a class is not offered unless there is sufficient enrollment to meet the cost of the course. Some states do provide funding for required high school courses on an average daily attendance basis. But more often courses are paid for on a tuition arrangement. Such an arrangement creates many problems for the summer school administrator. A commitment to hiring summer staff often cannot be made until the first day of class, when it is determined how many students actually show up and pay their tuition.

If the school district charges tuition, then there should be a plan for the tuition to be paid by installments and for a tuition waiver system for those parents who are unable to pay all or part of the tuition. Students who are not promoted should not be retained a year because their parents could not pay summer school tuition. However, the taxpayer must be kept in mind, and therefore all possible attempts should be made to secure state and federal aid for summer school.

Transportation

Bus transportation for summer school may be paid for by the state, the district, the student, or a combination of the three. In some city districts, the students may be able to ride the city buses to schools at special rates.

Since there are not enough summer school students to justify the complete bus service normally provided, the buses can be scheduled to make stops at convenient central locations. This eliminates extensive bus routing and conserves fuel. Of course, some districts provide no buses, and students must arrange for their own transportation.

Supplies and Equipment

One of the most frustrating aspects of summer school is the lack of adequate supplies and equipment. Because classes are not firmed up until the last moment, it is difficult to determine kinds and amounts of supplies and equipment needed. One large district had a policy of picking up all duplicating equipment for cleaning and repair as soon as school was out. Needless to say the summer school teacher in that district wrote a lot of material on the chalkboards. Since normal channels for requisitioning supplies do not function during the summer, the administrator must anticipate needs and see that adequate supplies and equipment are available.

Record Keeping

Summer school brings together students whose school records are in many different school buildings. Each student's grades, anecdotal records, etc., must get back to his or her official file. This is very important since students may be promoted or retained depending upon their achievement in summer school. For some high school students, graduation depends on complete records of their summer school work.

Public Relations

If summer school is to be accepted and financed by the community, it must be publicized as an ongoing part of the total educational program. David J. Wren cites some good public relations ideas for summer school:

1. Students are your best public relations agents. Youngsters who say that summer school is a "snap" can harm the program. Planned lessons should prevent this.

2. Write press releases before, during, and after the session. Pictorial layouts are very effective attention-getters during or after the summer session.

3. Print colorful brochures about the summer school program, which the guidance staff can distribute to potential students in May or June.

4. Stress how important the program is to the community. It offers credit make-up and enrichment courses; it is not a luxury to be cut at budget time.

A good summer school does not happen by accident. Much time and effort is needed to plan an educationally sound program. The summer school administrator is the key person in making it work.

Conclusion

Summer schools offer a rich opportunity to provide needed services and experiences for young people. For the student who needs additional assistance, for the ambitious student, and for the gifted student the summer school program can do what there is never enough time to do in the regular school year.

Summer schools have come a long way, but there is much work to be done. Hopefully, the ideas in this fastback will provide a "new look" for the summer school.

References

1. Massie J. Richmond, Jr., and Jack D. Riegel, "Current Status of the Extended School Year Movement," *Phi Delta Kappan* (March 1974): 490-492.
2. Clarence A. Schoenfeld and Neil Schmitz, *Year-Round Education* (Madison, Wisconsin: Dembar Educational Research Services, Inc., 1964), p. 36.
3. Chris Pipho, "Minimum Competency Testing in 1978: A Look at State Standards," *Phi Delta Kappan* (May 1978): 585.
4. Saroj Sutaria, "A Summer Program for Children with Learning Disabilities," *Journal of Learning Disabilities* (March 1979): 58-59.
5. Clair L. Koons, "Nonpromotion: A Dead-End Road," *Phi Delta Kappan* (May 1977): 701-702.
6. Charles Henry Keyes, *Progress Through the Grades of City Schools.* (New York: Bureau of Publications, Teachers College, Columbia University, 1911).
7. Department of Education, *A Directory of Summer Programs for Gifted Children: A Partial Listing of National Options* (Mars Hill, N.C.: Mars Hill College, 1979), pp. 1-23.
8. Anthony W. Scola, "Year-Round School," *NASSP Bulletin* 54 (March 1970): 83-84.
9. Roger E. Russell and Charles J. Fazzaro, "A New Look at the Year-Round School," *Clearinghouse* (December 1973): 196.
10. Sol Levine, "The John Dewey High School Adventure," in William Van Til, ed., *Curriculum: Quest for Relevance* 2nd ed. (Boston: Houghton Mifflin Co., 1974), p. 156.
11. J. Jackson Barnette, "Proposed, An Energy-Saving Education Calendar," *Phi Delta Kappan* (November 1978): 248.
12. Harold G. Shane and Owen N. Nelson, "What Will the Schools Become?", in William Van Til, ed., *Curriculum: Quest for Relevance,* 2nd ed. (Boston: Houghton Mifflin Co., 1974), p. 408.
13. David J. Wren, "Tips for the Summer School Administrator," *NASSP Newsletter* 26 (May 1979): 5.

Fastback Titles *(Continued from back cover)*

98. The Future of Teacher Power in America
99. Collective Bargaining in the Public Schools
100. How to Individualize Learning
101. Winchester: A Community School for the Urbanvantaged
102. Affective Education in Philadelphia
103. Teaching with Film
104. Career Education: An Open Door Policy
105. The Good Mind
106. Law in the Curriculum
107. Fostering a Pluralistic Society Through Multi-Ethnic Education
108. Education and the Brain
109. Bonding: The First Basic in Education
110. Selecting Instructional Materials
111. Teacher Improvement Through Clinical Supervision
112. Places and Spaces: Environmental Psychology in Education
113. Artists as Teachers
114. Using Role Playing in the Classroom
115. Management by Objectives in the Schools
116. Declining Enrollments: A New Dilemma for Educators
117. Teacher Centers—Where, What, Why?
118. The Case for Competency-Based Education
119. Teaching the Gifted and Talented
120. Parents Have Rights, Too!
121. Student Discipline and the Law
122. British Schools and Ours
123. Church-State Issues in Education
124. Mainstreaming: Merging Regular and Special Education
125. Early Field Experiences in Teacher Education
126. Student and Teacher Absenteeism
127. Writing Centers in the Elementary School
128. A Primer on Piaget
129. The Restoration of Standards: The Modesto Plan
130. Dealing with Stress: A Challenge for Educators
131. Futuristics and Education
132. How Parent-Teacher Conferences Build Partnerships
133. Early Childhood Education: Foundations for Lifelong Learning
134. Teaching about the Creation/Evolution Controversy
135. Performance Evaluation of Educational Personnel
136. Writing for Education Journals
137. Minimum Competency Testing
138. Legal Implications of Minimum Competency Testing
139. Energy Education: Goals and Practices
140. Education in West Germany: A Quest for Excellence
141. Magnet Schools: An Approach to Voluntary Desegregation
142. Intercultural Education
143. The Process of Grant Proposal Development
144. Citizenship and Consumer Education: Key Assumptions and Basic Competencies
145. Migrant Education: Teaching the Wandering Ones
146. Controversial Issues in Our Schools
147. Nutrition and Learning
148. Education in the USSR
149. Teaching with Newspapers: The Living Curriculum
150. Population, Education, and Children's Futures
151. Bibliotherapy: The Right Book at the Right Time
152. Educational Planning for Educational Success
153. Questions and Answers on Moral Education
154. Mastery Learning
155. The Third Wave and Education's Futures
156. Title IX: Implications for Education of Women
157. Elementary Mathematics: Priorities for the 1980s
158. Summer School: A New Look
159. Education for Cultural Pluralism: Global Roots Stew
160. Pluralism Gone Mad

PDK Fastback Series Titles

1. Schools Without Property Taxes: Hope or Illusion?
2. The Best Kept Secret of the Past 5,000 Years: Women Are Ready for Leadership in Education
3. Open Education: Promise and Problems
4. Performance Contracting: Who Profits Most?
6. How Schools Can Apply Systems Analysis
7. Busing: A Moral Issue
8. Discipline or Disaster?
9. Learning Systems for the Future
10. Who Should Go to College?
11. Alternative Schools in Action
12. What Do Students Really Want?
13. What Should the Schools Teach?
14. How to Achieve Accountability in the Public Schools
15. Needed: A New Kind of Teacher
16. Information Sources and Services in Education
17. Systematic Thinking about Education
18. Selecting Children's Reading
19. Sex Differences in Learning to Read
20. Is Creativity Teachable?
21. Teachers and Politics
22. The Middle School: Whence? What? Whither?
23. Publish: Don't Perish
24. Education for a New Society
25. The Crisis in Education Is Outside the Classroom
26. The Teacher and the Drug Scene
28. Education for a Global Society
29. Can Intelligence Be Taught?
30. How to Recognize a Good School
31. In Between: The Adolescent's Struggle for Independence
32. Effective Teaching in the Desegregated School
33. The Art of Followership (What Happened to the Indians?)
34. Leaders Live with Crises
35. Marshalling Community Leadership to Support the Public Schools
36. Preparing Educational Leaders: New Challenges and New Perspectives
37. General Education: The Search for a Rationale
38. The Humane Leader
39. Parliamentary Procedure: Tool of Leadership
40. Aphorisms on Education
41. Metrication, American Style
42. Optional Alternative Public Schools
43. Motivation and Learning in School
44. Informal Learning
45. Learning Without a Teacher
46. Violence in the Schools: Causes and Remedies
47. The School's Responsibility for Sex Education
48. Three Views of Competency-Based Teacher Education: I Theory
49. Three Views of Competency-Based Teacher Education: II University of Houston
50. Three Views of Competency-Based Teacher Education: III University of Nebraska
51. A University for the World: The United Nations Plan
52. Oikos, the Environment and Education
53. Transpersonal Psychology in Edu
54. Simulation Games for the Classr
55. School Volunteers: Who Needs Th
56. Equity in School Financing: Full
57. Equity in School Financing: Distr Equalizing
58. The Computer in the School
59. The Legal Rights of Students
60. The Word Game: Improving Comm
61. Planning the Rest of Your Life
62. The People and Their Schools: Co Participation
63. The Battle of the Books: Kanawha
64. The Community as Textbook
65. Students Teach Students
66. The Pros and Cons of Ability Gro
67. A Conservative Alternative Schoo A+ School in Cupertino
68. How Much Are Our Young People Story of the National Assessment
69. Diversity in Higher Education: Re the Colleges
70. Dramatics in the Classroom: Maki Come Alive
71. Teacher Centers and Inservice Edu
72. Alternatives to Growth: Education Stable Society
73. Thomas Jefferson and the Educati New Nation
74. Three Early Champions of Educati Franklin, Benjamin Rush, and Noa
75. A History of Compulsory Educatio
76. The American Teacher: 1776-1976
77. The Urban School Superintendency and a Half of Change
78. Private Schools: From the Puritan Present
79. The People and Their Schools
80. Schools of the Past: A Treasury o
81. Sexism: New Issue in American Ed
82. Computers in the Curriculum
83. The Legal Rights of Teachers
84. Learning in Two Languages

84S. Learning in Two Languages (Span

85. Getting It All Together: Confluent
86. Silent Language in the Classroom
87. Multiethnic Education: Practices a
88. How a School Board Operates
89. What Can We Learn from the Schoo
90. Education in South Africa
91. What I've Learned About Values Ed
92. The Abuses of Standardized Testin
93. The Uses of Standardized Testing
94. What the People Think About Their Gallup's Findings
95. Defining the Basics of American Ed
96. Some Practical Laws of Learning
97. Reading 1967-1977: A Decade of C Promise

(Continued on inside back cove

See inside back cover for pr